KRUSH:
ER & the Strokes

THE SURVIVOR OF A STROKE

Keith "Krusher" Rush

KRUSH: ER & the Strokes
The Survivor of a Stroke

First Edition: 2022

ISBN: 9781524318482
ISBN eBook: 9781524328450

© of the text:
    Keith "Krusher" Rush

© Layout, design and production of this edition: 2022
EBL

All rights reserved. No part of this publication may be reproduced, distributed, or transmitted in any form or by any means, including photocopying, recording, or other electronic or mechanical methods, without the prior written permission of the Publisher.

*This memoir-writing is dedicated to Ms. Janice Marie Crawford Rush my saint & my living Angel. Thanks Ma, love u! (I put my blood, sweat, & tears in this one ma, well * no tears for me just yet, lol ~happy tears~)*

(Please feel free to donate, information is located in the end.)

KRUSH: ER & THE STROKES

THE SURVIVOR OF A STROKE

The story of Keith "Krusher" Rush & returning the love by caring for his disabled mother

Hello good people my name is Keith "Krusher" Rush & due to the astronomical costs of my prescribed medication & dr offices bills to keep me & my disabled mother alive, it is becoming egregiously abhorrent & cost defective for dealing with all of our medical issues... I'm talking $1,200 bucks a month in total for us just to stay alive? REALLY? The in general amount of donated monies goals from my previous GoFund Me account is set for $10,000 dollars for the whole year but it anything would suffice & so much more than the 10K a year is needed but anything would really help. it also would go towards transportation to & from dr visits. vehicle maintenance, wheelchair maintenance, & some home repair maintenance (from which the wheelchair puts scratches on the walls & floors & it stresses the floor board underneath the house-from some bad work done, I explain more in the story about the bad contractor).

Idk what it is, Healthcare it just ain't right. & The reason why it's so messy is bc the healthcare in Georgia is so flawed when it comes to healthcare. It's way different in Carolina... From state to state it should be equal everywhere u go... tell me, how does this happen? One area u can get something & when ur in another u can't..America, we gotta fix this. This ain't right, this is silly & ridiculous!

My mom is not the type of person that will ask for any help or she would consider it to be begging, & she is very prideful, & I am too, yet she is so humble but I see that these medical bills, dr visits, & prescriptions are getting extremely way out of hand & we need the relief, but she needs the help IMHO & she won't just say it... She never ever ever will say she needs help... she's always been like that. well, her son will say it for her & that's my cue, lol She raised me that way too, but enough is enough with these medical bills & stuff. She would not even approve of me saying or doing anything that would ask or solicit any help... (BTW-I will tell her about this later though, not now in the midst or in the beginning of me organizing relief efforts, but I'm sure she will hop on board & catch up later once it's up & rolling & I tell her about it... I can hear her questioning me in my head right now saying such things as in, "What makes ur stroke so hot topic? Or why is it such a big deal?" For I got a good answer right here, I feel the need to share the story, a rare look & have insight into my life. This is my story, this is my song. Just to give you some insights about my story, here we go,

As I am sitting here and listening to the telephone conference conversations between the two assorting all of the business with Medicare I think about the word care out of Medicare. Mama is the ultimate one who cares... She is the care in Medicare. Is it still being called Medicare, it should be called "Mama-care" cuz when it is time to shine she shines so bright! What would I do without her handling the business. She can't move around as much nowadays but she knows how to pick up that phone just like her dad "Big John" John Ellis Crawford Sr. (A true trailblazer, one of a kind might I add) but I don't know and I don't want to find out right now either of her not enjoying a reward. U see, from a woman who ain't never WON anything in her life, for, the ultimate caregiver in my life, took the angelic angel that God has placed in my life, he put his hands on her big time too by the way, they're not enough words in the dictionary to describe my mother.

There's not much more I can truly keep on saying thank u &. already know "I just love me some mama" (I tell her that 50-11 times a day, lol) * I stay forever dropping "love bombs" on her, well on everybody... I got this motto I go by, "ELE" = ~ Everybody Loves Everybody ~ & now on to the story:

Krusher had a stroke! Based on a TRUE story!

Alright! Let's start this bad boy off in 2009. It started off as a good year. I am a stand-up kinda bruhtha, tall, strong, omega man, I was feeling fine in '09 & then it quickly turned into a "uhh ohh" moment... I had lost weight... 175 pounds to be exact... Bought a brand new house, had two nice cars & pickup truck... I was a walking 6'9" tall African American BMW, which means BLACK MAN WORKING! Lol

Everything was on the up & up, having a real successful life for myself. All I was looking for is my Queen (& mama sure was pressing me super hard for a wife & making some kids) & she still is to this day is doing so but it's even harder for me nowadays bc what would u have to offer a woman in a relationship... It's too much work for her. That's what she would say. & yes it true that I've been told that too but what do u do? oh well, u live & u learn. but never mind all that noise, my reward is on the way. but before that I got a bigger problem ahead... & oh boy here comes a big storm...

Here comes a "Big Uhh Ohh"

I am a stroke survivor. I know that a lot of people in the world have a stroke but Here is what had happened to me, & just a little about my history. See what had happened was, On August 29, 2009 I had my first stroke. I was released with some meds & stuff after 1week in... I got discharged & then 2 weeks later I was admitted again after my 2nd stroke at University hospital in Augusta, Ga & after my 2nd stroke, I was then told after my MRI that this would be a tricky surgery. None of the doctors in the area could perform this operation & blood vessels in my brain were tangled up, dripping 2.17cm on my brain & the world's top neurologist Dr. Daniel Barrow, who is a professor of medicine at Emory University could squeeze me in for an emergency surgery. So I went in for urgent surgery & about 9 & a half hours later, I had my 3rd stroke while actually on the operating room table... I was in a coma & stayed in a coma for about 4months & when the doctor came out he told my family what had happened during surgery which basically saying that I had an AVM in the brain & I had complications from AVM surgery which caused me to have blurred vision, limited usage of all of my limbs... limited speech as well. Really sometimes I would need a translator or subtitles for people to understand me. In which I understand it. & especially if u don't talk with me on a daily basis, ur gonna ask me to repeat myself or agree but I can read the muscles in ur face reacting toward a conversation topic being discussed... Fun fact, did u know that it is really cheaper to smile rather than frown... u use about 11 muscles in ur face & up to 15 when u frown...

I used to always hear it from my third grade teacher from Thomson Elementary Miss. Karen Wicker, "it's cheaper to smile than it is to frown." It really is, don't ever disagree with a teacher, Way to go faculty & staff of the great Thomson Elementary. Y'all are awesome over there. "Each one, Teach one" & she did & for that I have to shout u out & salute

Being placed on a ventilator is no fun. I don't remember anything of it at all except for I would respond when people would talk to me. I was in a coma in ICU at Emory for four months, in a total of five different hospitals from Augusta to Atlanta for seven or eight months... it was almost like an act of Congress to get me admitted in over at Walton... my dear friend Mrs. Laurie Ott & Estelle Parsley with Lynnsey Baker hooked me up with that & some. Shawn Jones helped ur boy. out for real ... I did forget to mention that strangely I had lost 175 pounds before I had this stroke. It came off of me effortlessly... I wondered how & why was this happening... Why was I losing the weight so fast? At first it was cool... I looked real good... Even though this weigh loss was noticeable by many. I even was asked by a police investigator who hadn't seen me in a while, we was at the scene of a crime & he said "Krusher, don't let me catch u on 5th street buying no crack!" I would reply back, "Nah bruh, that's not me, I say NO to drugs, this all me, homie." But I did it for the original intent was to lose bout 20 pounds & to have this chick I previously dated to see what the hell she was missing out on, but I told her, "Aye girl, lol, u know it's hard trying to be skinny, I'm just preserving my sexy" lol ... My family & I believe that it was one of Gods blessings, it made it easier for me to be carried around at first, I say at first bc A. It made me lighter to carry & B. I did not eat any solid foods for about a whole entire year... A tube had to be placed in my stomach to inject liquid nutrients in... I could not have solid foods for some time but when I got the chance to do so, it was not anything stopping me from food. Oh & all that weight I lost, about 100 pounds of it started to creep back in. & everyone in my family said at the time it was ok. I was bones, not skin & bones, just bones.... & nah I don't have any pictures to show it to u, just trust me, it was badder than BAD!

I looked like a skeleton exhibit! I never did any weight loss pills or surgery or nothing like that, all I did was exercise more, change up my eating habits. Fruits & veggies of course. Lots of rabbit food, lol I ate a lot more canned tuna (ask Lynnsey Baker, who rode in the car with it, lol) The last year has been different on the diet as far as the price of eating healthy hasn't been so good in my point of view. I hate to be so cynical about being in a area that's a food desert but it's like we could be worse. It's also expensive eating healthy too & these Dr. Bills & stuff sure not helping in expenditures.

Don't cry mama! & she never did either. To this day I never did cry as well., & man that was in 2009. I see where I get my strength, resilience, & endurance from. All my toughness from my mama. But during that time. It was very sad, emotional, & so much to think about... As my ma would say "she did not have any time to cry, she had business to take care of."She has been with me from day 1. Everyone else was really hurt & crying so much, rightfully so, it was about to be a sad & tragic ending at the young age of 27 with so much more life to live. Wherever, whenever, & whatever she has been there for every step. It is so selfless of her to mention it to me that she would rather it had been her that it would have happened to bc she felt that a piece of my life had been taken away & used as an experience... Most people don't make it through. I did, I still am blinking & breathing... & looking at the big picture I'm still here. Someone else in the world has it much worse than me... I'm blessed, black, & highly favored!

They thought that they were fixing to lose me. Really, they did... Even the doctor did. The rigor mortis starts to set in once u expire... I leaned that at an early age when we had a family funeral home, my uncle Ronnie Crawford told Dr. Barrow to please keep my nephew alive by any means necessary sir... We need him here on earth, blinking & breathing... Then there would have been one other call to our honorary cousin D. T Brown Funeral Home in Thomson Ga. The family didn't have to make that call. It sounded to me like they were almost on the verge. But it's good that I'm talking about D. T Brown funeral home throughout this book... Because I'm sure that would've been one call my family dreaded to make, even though we're "kinfolk" & the services of D. T Brown funeral home wasn't needed yet. Thank goodness the good lord ain't done with me on earth yet... I'm still here, RIGHT! & when he calls me, I will answer. Oh & I'll be somewhere listening for my name (Deacon Joe Jackson favorite song) But I kept on having fluid on the brain. My kidneys had shut down. They thought I was going to need dialysis for the rest of my life...

On top of that, I'm NEVER to walk, drive, play musical instruments, sing, etc... or so that's what the doctor said. & if u think I'm resting on that then I say "don't believe me, just watch" Also I had a pulmonary embolism traveling from my legs they put a shunt or stint in which incapacitated my lungs, I actually had a collapsed lung... All my meds to keep me alive after this is 10 to 12 pills each day. Not all at once... I know that's a lot but I thank God so much for this cause it could be so much worse... talk about petrified, yes indeed I was bc when i was in a coma I dreamt I spent time with deceased. But ur boy did have a sweet dream in there too! I don't know who, what, when, where or how... ohhhh weeeee! I'll just leave it at this "Girl, stand by, I'm coming for her! (Please believe that! GUARANTEED)

I go through wheelchairs like little toys...

Maybe bc I am a big dude was the reason why the wheelchair's chair was stressed so much... Well i am 6' 9" nearly 400pds. I know that's a massive human being. It reads out like an intimidating wrestlers walking to the ring with Mr Antrone Brewer Da' Fireman ringing me in with me doing the Ric Flair nature boy drip, "Wooooooo" lol! I used to be the biggest fan of wrestling as a kid.

Speaking of me putting a figure four leg lock on someone, (that was Flair's signature move), Mr. Bill will fix it is a scammer, I wrote to the BBB about him, here it is...

I was easily triggered today when there is a problem that occurred in my home, & another contractor came in & see where it was a sham job done from the beginning, & now I have to deal with it by getting it fixed with more money being spent by me for a whole another person & I have to do this bc of this low life, shady carpenter named Bill @ Mr. Bill-will-fix-it... bc of his shoddy ness & contempt of not even doing the job lying to my mama over the telephone saying that everything is finish knowing our handicapped situation kept us from looking & observing. Him going through her & not me bc he was trying to get over on a woman... & apparently we're not the first clients he's screwed over... that ain't right brother, u won't get a blessing that way.

Nonetheless...

I will spare most of the detail, honestly not enough words would fit in this comments section of the BBB, although I wish I did have more time to unleash on the unsatisfactory work done and to tell this story, but he knows who he scammed, schemed, & preyed upon. 2 disabled people but karma i keep on telling u about karma & again ur talking to two children of God & u might just want to be careful it's going to come back to get u bruh. God don't like ugly. It's not righteous at all what was done & Gods got it... God sees & He knows... & God bless u Bill... We hold no grudge or animosity...

I will say

Mr. Bill will fix it in Augusta Ga, 0 stars,

I'm not a star but I ain't gonna never eva, eva, EVA get outta the wheelchair, is what would be said... I don't believe that at all. Ur only wasting ur money. I don't think so... ur only spending all ur time & energy for what. It ain't helping u... out of all of that talking, Man "F- that noise" honestly, u know I ain't hearing that noise. Mannn, during this illness I've heard NO so many times & in so many shapes & forms, it goes Noooo, Nope, Nuope, Nah bruh, Nuhh Uhh, No, No, No (In Deborah Cox voice) lol btw, we played that song at a talent show & blew the roof off the auditorium*cherished memories last a lifetime. Anyway back to it. it's crazy cause all my little nieces & nephews like riding & playing in my wheelchair & others like to sit in the wheelchair when I'm not using it, BUT I'm the one not trying to making it a permanent fixture, I'm tryna "POOF! Be gone" with this chair but until then I thank GOD for the chair, it gets my big ole butt from point A to point B (slowly but surely), all I need now is a CD player & some speakers, lol I forgot it ain't CD's no more, it's all Spotify & pandora playlist nowadays.

Speaking of music, Ain't no mo play in Ga. literally... it just seemed like when I moved back to Georgia it literally was like that... Shout out to Pastor Troy. We went hard for P. T Cruiser in high school and I still show love til dis day and almost daily I listen to the greatest underground independent artists EVER... (hands down) Superheroes gotta have their theme music, mine is "Pastor-Disaster" PASTOR TROY! *We Ready! soooo, I am shooting my shot with some of everybody and I mean some of EVERYBODY (Women) Lol At first I thought, oh bummer, Should I just stop what I do, am I embarrassing myself, cause I know I ain't "Butt-Booty-Ugly" LOL. But geeeeezzz u chose that over ME? WOWWW! I get turnt pretty quick like ice cream sitting in a car on a hot summer day.

Lol, ohh welllll, on to the next, I don't skip a beat, I play the drums too, lol... God will bless me abundantly one day, so I fret not, it's all to the good, it is what it is. & that's just the way I been looking at it since I been in Middle School. Actually I've never had a girlfriends-relationship in my life, I've been looking but never found Mrs. Rush. I've been in a few "situation-ish" or some "situation-ships" but never the real deal. Henceforward the name Krusher... I always got a krush on somebody's daughter. Lol ... nah actually that's my real name. My government name is Keith Rush. U put the K & Rush together added with an ER. Whoop there it is, lol ... Shout out to Johanne Davis for coming up with a clever way in a newsroom with that! I forever appreciate that sistah!

Did I mention that I am the Chief Photojournalist & Satellite Truck Operator for the #1 News in the whole wide world, (well Augusta, Ga) that is, lol WRDW-TV 12 CBS/NBC Augusta, Ga. I used to be the cameraman with my reporter, do feature stories or packages, run their live shots locally or anywhere in the world sports or weather we would do it all. I remember Vernon Blue, Johanne Davis, Domonique Benn, Tom & Moody (RIP), Tammy Greene, Melissa Tune, Big Sammy Sam, Brandon Neal, TJ Wilson, Tim-Bo Strong, Jay & Bonita Jeffries power couple of the year, Shalanda, Jocelyn Manor (she got married), (But not married to my next homie) Marc Willis, Alicia Benjamin, like 50 women name Stephanie, but Brightie comes into my mind Dr. Stephanie Brightharp-Cartwright & Richard "Richie-Rich" Rogers on the night shift. We all used to hold it down like a "fat man on a seesaw" lol

But back to the music side of things, I was pretty good. I could play music by hearing it (or play by ear) sight reading or sheet reading music. Outstanding at music nonetheless... my music appreciation skills are still sharp. Weird music fun fact: i can tell u the song that then DJ is about to play within the first 3 seconds of a mix's. I don't know why or how, or what use it's for but ok, I'll take it... but I say this not to diminish myself by using the talents wasted away any bc we had a few other real musicians who do this for a living & they are even better.... I mean playing with top ranking artist & such. Sidebar- Local or traveling musicians we ALL (M.B.'s) really most definitely have made an impact in whatever we do for a living. & just to think, what brought us together was a few reasons but it was mainly the music. But back to it now. Really it went for just a side gig or just a hobby for me... I wasn't worried about money at the time, I had a great full time job so music wasn't a real source of my income, although it could have been a source. I just felt like I could use my talents as a hobby, or something just for fun, I'm sure I would be blessed in other form, it's all about showing some love & just do it, & not looking for nothing in return. That's why God might have given me the gift of music... "I got 5 on it" (In my Luniz voice) *I remember I had a tuba solo in band growing up. Me, Crenshaw & the boys with our jam session... Critty was the boy genius alongside me, Freddy, Keven (RIP), Nard, Stantwan, Spencer, Brian, Shamarcus, Corey, Terrance, & Pooh... But anyway I play the tuba, trombone, baritone, drums, & I dabbled with the trumpet (So I used to have that baboon butt lip

like a long time ago all the freaking time) Lol *if u play horns for the first time in a "Hot Minute" u know what I'm talking about ... I used to could sing lead just a lil' bit in the church choir. Actually Bro. Anthony Ferris used the Swiss Army analogy on me... with a regular knife u just have one knife, u see with a Swiss Army knife u have a plethora of different types of knives...Yes the Jack of all trades. I play & do so much musically I could be compared to a Swiss Army knife bc I play all different instruments but my voice box has been shattered & my lungs were capacitated with a blood clot going through. Whoa it even sounds bad re reading this whole entire story so far. It's ok though, I still make a little noise doing something in the auxiliaries section or in percussion sections... it don't stop, that's what my homie Keven Hill (RIP) would say... He was my childhood friend... We actually were in a group growing up called "The Mama's Boys" staying on the main topic of these prescriptions/diagnosis but man I just have to say, we were all A-W-E-S-O-M-E, I mean mannnnnn, talented, gifted, amazing musically, we brought joy to many people's ears, we all played by ear... bad to the bones we were so ahead of our time musically, especially in '99-2000, lol now whenever u heard Juvenile say that part, 1-2, u know what to do... dance floor now, lol. Church events, wedding, funerals, talent showcases, etc. anything musically, ur face was in the place to hear the Mama's Boys & we were L-E-G-E-N-D-A-R-Y in most of Georgia the CSRA... & we went to Arkansas too... Even in or 255-piece high school marching band we all were the standouts in music especially... we traveled to Detroit, Canada Mia for parades & stuff. When we pulled up we would roll deep. I'm talking like 8 or 9 buses... pulling like 2 trailers filled to the brim with equipment. We were the "Good-Badd Boys" of our era... I mean we straight up kilt'ed, not killed it, KILLT'ED IT! Band, yep I mean Band, Band. Lol When I tell u our band was good, we got a whole lot of trophies, medals, awards, plaques superior rankings hanging... Even still till this day a few of us still got talent & a few of us M. B's still can play, u know it man we the "M. B's 4 life!", where ever we go though, in the words of our brother Keven Hill, "IT DON'T STOP"

*RIP- long live Keven "drummer boy" Hill... (That boy was FIYA on them drums!)

Back to my diagnosis...

Wow on paper these diagnoses are a lot, yes it is... losing all or most of ur abilities is better than losing ur life. I will take it for sure... Every doctor's office I go to they tell me I'm so lucky! Lucky to just even be here... they all stop especially after they read all these diagnoses to themselves, & I notice "That Face Jerk" every time, it never gets old, kinda used to it by now. The "WOW" factor & all I can say is "Look at GOD"

God is good _____, & All the time _____! He only has me here for a reason. I don't know what that reason may be but I can only imagine & speculate to show my fellow bro's & sis's what he could do. Even though sickness attacks the body it can be a moment of silence or a moment of u to jus. B. t shut it on down. Speaking on shuttingk down COVID-19 was a hot mess... a lot of people I knew were here today, gone tomorrow... so tragic to see, I lost two real tight friends, one was young (39) & the other was an elderly friend (87), my auntie *but not related. I miss her dearly. I still keep up with her family & I've never even seen them so I wouldn't even know what or who to look for... But I couldn't even go to either one of those funerals bc it was in the thick of COVID & I just couldn't risk it... I could have went but doctors had real fears of loss of life would have been real easier for the virus to catch me slipping... (& I'm paranoid) I don't get caught slipping. No surprises here! Well u can try but trust me, I'm very observant, I got them "camera eyes" after all i am the Chief Photographer/Satellite Truck Operator for the #1 news in Augusta, Ga. WRDW-TV

CBS/NBC News.

I used to go some of everywhere, I enjoyed it too. It's what I always wanted to do... Being sick is super expensive when you go out to say like you go to football game, concert or a comedy show it's like super expensive cuz you pay for two tickets or u have to partner up with someone who is going & it's a whole lot of mess, work, & coordination, & it's hard for somebody that is your age that is single to go out with as a buddy you know because you don't have anybody to take You anywhere. It's like that & that's the way it is unfortunately. "Ur best bet is to stay at home", is what ma & grandma would say.

During COVID it felt like Groundhog Day! Everything was the same thing over & over again. I found myself turning into an introvert. If I look at the bigger picture I'm really a ambivert... It was a hard time for everyone but if ur reading this then congratulations u made it. It's life & in my life for me it felt like I was on a house arrest or at least the house arrest I've seen on TV. (I don't like this vibe tho, but it's all the truth) I couldn't go nowhere or be around people for like a year & a half. See, I'm extremely grateful to have a roof & a bed, & it was just a lived experience that culminated into not going anywhere or doing anything for about 18 months... When Trevor Noah from The Daily Show calls it The Socially Distancing Show, I really am, I had to, my life depended on me socially distancing. I was susceptible to this virus. Technically it would find me quicker than it would an average person... & then let's say if I went or, & caught it or another person passes it to me then I prolly wouldn't make it so that's a big ole' fat NUOPE for me... U won't see me nowhere during the time... I will say it was a rough time for all families but we vaccinated & ready to go... At least we keep on keeping on even though. Or at least until the next bill smacks u dead in the face. But the best thing I have done with all this time is started working on writings, I don't know what it was for at first but I seem to know lately.

I hate talking about all the little things that come out as negative but it's all so true...

FRIENDS, how many of us have them...

A song so true made by "Whodini" MAN oh MAN when u get sick, some of ur real friends turn into just regular people who know u. Or who know of u... that's just how it is. it makes u question urself & ur friendship was it really a friendship anyways... Some home boys have stayed down for sure... We ride or die for real... Call each other on birthdays, know their kids names & stuff..True "friendos" indeed, who always stay down, & pause for the cause. Now that right there, that's the kind of friends I'm talking about ... I'll do anything in my power for my brother &; sister... they got their true fairytale love story & I'm glad to be along for their ride... (& it was all orchestrated & instigated by ME in our high school days, lol) Cause they real & they true with it. Shoutout to Dr. Chris & Kwanza Atkinson

But people have said unfortunately when ur sick or when u pass away mostly everyone will forget about u. My phones used to ring of the hook, like a telethon... i remember I had two cellular phones, a pager, home phone, & a fax machine in the office. In the truck there were 6 box stationary lines, with 2 outside rotary lines where u can patch other lines through. Needless to say, I was the man in charge. The Big Chief. The head, the leader, the one u could come to who would help. Now that I'm the one who needs the help where u at friends? People know u when they see u, but until then Nope... See what had happened was.idk I had millions of friends before when I first got sick... I mean a couple ride or die, day ones klick, or homies but as the world turns, chapters quickly turn & u can't force no one to love u even though they say they do... I'm just saying... I'm just keeping it real! Remember that sickness is in everyone, u'll see in the future... I'm not the only one who notices the phone never rings for me no more... but it always gets noticed that it's me doing all the loving... I remember in band from high school we used to jam out to "Gimmie Some Lovin' "well that song is in my mind now bc that's all a bro wants a little of that Agape Love reciprocated. & don't forget, most people or everyone gets sick or old before death. Do unto others as u would want them to do upon u... U do have some really good souls out there in the world... Some "friendos" that wholeheartedly care for u... Want to see u be great! I could name a heap load of people that are good to me... Real good friends that if I were to pick up the phone they would be happy to do whatever... Some family who look out for ur boi.. I got some uncles who come through, what more can I say bout us Crawford men. (My last name ain't Crawford but ain't no doubt about it, it's in my blood for sure. Lol) So I hate to be such a downer, but it's definitely not like that! None of those things are true when it comes to whether u have someone to have ur back. But I will say people Most of ur day ones turn into spectators or associates... I understand it tho. People gotta live their lives though, but don't be mad when I turn my chapter & u ain't involved... I hate to be like this... it's sad to me but moving right along, this train don't stop, #ChooCHOO!

One thing about your sickness, I don't have to pay my massive student loan debt. Well yet, while I'm impelled within. The collectors stopped ringing me. My mom and I were both in the car coming back from the doctor and we both agreed if we could swap these circumstances out we would obliged but we know that it's all up to the man above who put us in this situation. He's got it all under control. He's got me here to spread and share my story, so I shall do so.

With being disabled comes the many cost of repairs. So many things need to be repaired, we had a guy who had done some remodeling to modify my handicapped home but he did a "sham" job, he is a "halfway modern day crook"is what I call him. A straight up "Buster from Augusta" name Mr. Bill- will-fix-it, he bamboozled & stole my mom's money by pmanipulation but "God don't like ugly", he will get u, & get u GOOD too. Please believe that karma's gonna get u buddy. Especially taking advantage of the sick & elderly people. I'm a man, look me in the eyes bro & he even had the nerve to go around town, boast, brag, & rave unwittingly to my kinfolk. Don't worry he will give u 5 minutes. Please believe that! Other than that. So this is some of the reasons I try not to even bother my mom with getting these things at the home repaired., I don't bother her bc I know that it will take a whole lot of money (like ma would say, "money u ain't got to fork over!")

Also, I meant to ask u do u have $3 million I can borrow from you? LOL that should be pocket change for u big dawg. That's what I would tell u! Do u think I will ever make $3 milly in my life?

Pfffffftttttt, lol. Hell naw. LOL! Too funny. It makes me laugh... lol. Just to even think if I had that kind of mullah what would I do. Hmmm? Put some on the bill for a nice/real vacation & then give the rest of it to ma, all for her. She deserves it. She put in all the work. She needs to be gifted for an outstanding and magnificent job she has done. I'll speak all of these blessings into existence... I just get frustrated when I hear ma doing the bills & I can't contribute... one day she will be rewarded & it don't take much for her either, just love & some acknowledgment... May the work she's done, speak for her! Knowing Ma, that's all she would accept, she's a giver, not a taker... That's who I definitely get that from. The loving, giving, nurturing, softer, thoughtfulness qualities are from her... DON'T get it twisted though, I'm a real MAN now though, I do have a softer side on me from my "MUM" (in my British pronunciation voice) lol

I know that the whole country is going through a tough time right now dealing with the economy and everything, but it's way more tougher on me right now, it's same as if my load is twice or three times more harder. & hopefully with me pushing this memoir out there, I can help out as much as possible.

Always look good coming out of the house

"Never let them see you sweat" is how the saying goes, well actually I do sweat a lot. Not like a normal person. I sweat just standing still, lately sitting still. I always wear a t-shirt up under my regular shirt. If I don't then I'm sweating through that shirt, please believe. It's been like that my whole life, I used to get picked on as a kid but ayeeee look at the man who I've become now, just look at me now!

You learn something new every day, in this case it was facts and numbers involving how many people in the country have been affected with an AVM stroke. About 200,000 people are affected with this kind of stroke. It can be a lifelong condition, or to me that's what they say I can do The impossible, I can see the invisible, because I know I got faith! So oh no I'm not going to speak losing the battle into existence. & I didn't know that men could get "UTI" now. Can u say hospital bills! those were some big hospital bills there, and bed sores, u get them a lot, u go through so much too, on the outside u look real good when stepping on the scene, but if u only knew the inside pain, it's kinda good when u have nice family or friends basically anyone who wanna do the simple things for you to help you out, it's all a blessing the way I look at it. All in all though when having those challenges I might have been losing that battle but I'm winning the war!

Now a challenge that I been through lately is that I have went through a lot of wheelchairs... At first I really couldn't help but wheelchairs are definitely not made for abig person. U gotta think, I'm 6' 9" almost 400 pds soaking wet, with a 18" inch shoe size. I tried to tell u earlier in the memoir I was a giant human being... imma lose some weight bc I'm on a mission. Man I would breakdown in them things like it was nothing. Oh no not bc I treated my chair bad, I treated it real good too. I kept it shining (if I could've I would've put some rims & beats galore, straight pimp my ride "Throw Some Deez On It") lol man nah. Just kidding... I'm just wanted a ride".

A heavy duty type of wheelchair but Medicare was really trippin'! Something that could get me from point A. B. & maybe even C. Lol

Healthcare for the disabled or people who are disenfranchised is THE ABSOLUTE WORST! (Period)

That's all I wanna say about that bc it's so negative I don't even want to get angry... I will say this, as soon as I'm back on my feet I'm immediately advocating for us... I'm coming for u government & big pharmaceutical & if big tech has anything to do with it too, well then u too!

But I would like to say, Health you need it, for your quality of life. It's a must, but once u get sick, and you start to have to depend on Medicare supplements man it's like a full-time job answering all the phones during normal business hours. If they don't call you cell phone they called the house phone then they email you. And they call you from all across the USA. I can tell you the number to all of the area called just about in the USA from because I get a call from everywhere in the country. When ur name goes in their database oh man they got u. U ask the telemarketing people to take ur name off the list but it seems like they call a lot more...

Man did I mention the negative & the positives of this illness. U know how on commercials they always read the side effects fast, well, do that with all this negative stuff...

- loss of life
- Wheelchair bound
- Neuropathy
- Slurred Speech
- Blurred Vision
- Blood Clots
- Lung Facilities Fracture
- Nerve Endings
- Sensations of something crawling up & down ur legs when u whine down at night.
- Bowel Incontenance
- Urinary incontenance
- Depression
- psoriasis
- kidney stones
- kidney failure
- kidney failure that requires dialysis
- High Prescription Meds
- Loneliness (mental health psyche)
- Feelings of being left out
- Feelings of being too slow

- Frequent Vomiting
- Bed Sores
- Body Sensation
- Emotional affects
- Blood Pressure Issues
- Night Sweats
- Night terrors
- Brittle Bones
- Skin tone deteriorated
- Non-Independence
- Non-Activity of limbs
- Non-nourishment of meals
- Problems digestion of solid foods which leads to more vomiting
- Sleepiness from medication
- volume controls in speech which is known as dysarthria
- a form of PBA (uncontrollable laughter)
- Aspirations in Sleep Studies

Wow I could see why no one wanted to deal with me unless they had too, Mama was right! I ain't normal! & u can't go everywhere & u can't get into everyone house… I will add too When you get cut you have to be very careful because the bleed out is real… u bleed a lot & it's very hard to stop the bleeding because it's so much.

Also you have to be mindful of the places that ur going too. U have to be aware and give assessable not that many places are handicap accessible places like barbershop or a churches or a business most places say they are but really they aren't even equipped for the handicapped. I mean it's not reasonable at most establishments. That's another reason why I stay home is bc most situations as simple as the question that always comes to my mind usually is where would you go if you had to go to the

But all in all the positives outweighs all of this "negative narrative stuff"

- At least ur alive (blinking & breathing)
- U got a bed to lay in.
- U got clothes on ur back.

Shoes on ur feet.
In ur right mind.

- V. I. P parking & u always get to park in front.
- V. I. P treatment everywhere u go.

& u always have a chair to sit in...

I wouldn't recommend anyone to have a stroke for any of the superlatives but if u do I would suggest u take full advantage of some of this it will help u in the long haul... in therapy they used to call me the Michael Jordan of a stroke. That's real good to be acknowledged as one of the greats... it speaks volumes into me just trying to get better.

Another thing about ur debilitating injury & why everyday feels like Groundhog Day, is ur invited but not really ur invited is the kinda vibe we get, I know, that's F'd up to the 3rd degree... if someone does that to u... it's like I'm a modern day Cinderella but I'm the Cinderella as a man.... It could be a movie someday... yeah, I'm too big or don't deserve to go anywhere in their eyes, For me it feels that way kind of.. sometimes not being taken care of but taken care of, if u know what I mean... it's life man. & no I'm not complaining about being mistreated at all. I have the best mother on this side of heaven... One who goes above & beyond. I wouldn't trade her for the world... I'm just sharing my stroke story... with all that said... Loneliness Happens to me constantly... It happens so much we kinda got used to the loneliness especially around the holidays. It's always chalked up to everyone wanna be with their own friends & family but what I would rebut "ain't we kin folk too?" I thought we were. Geez... It's always a problem with smooth transportation with a wheelchair too & not having a real strong-minded fella at the house to transport me or help mama out well it just ain't working out right for us. I know u already got me enough as a strong minded man but... u know what I mean... lol but yeah back to the loneliness part... people just wanna be a nice so they can save face when it comes down to being social... but we all know what's real?... I get it tho. To keep from causing confusion I would just rather have to stay at home..My grandma did tell me-that some of them friends aren't really ur friends & especially this sicknesses has proven that as a fact. U used to get a lot of invites to birthday parties, weddings, reunion parties, dinner parties, cookouts, etc. BUT ur invitation gets lost in the mail or some petty excuse usually would fly... & u wanna know how I know it's just BS is bc I'm sitting at a lower level, the projection & angles of ur body usually sends off signals, triggers, etc. & I hate talking about all this negative stuff but it's all true... it's even more stuff but it just has too much of a negative vibe to it, it ain't worth more time spent. So I can just leave it right there...

I can't believe it's so hard for me to get outta bed EVERY SINGLE DAY...

Into bed is very hard as well... Those "I'm falling & I can't get up" commercial is so true... Oh man, how true it is... it's happened to me so I would know firsthand. & even getting in the bed for sleep is tough but u can muster up enough strength to get in there... There have been so many times. Scratch that all the time, when ur sick it feels like u got like a million pounds attached to u... Especially when do therapy or other activities... u can't hardly play or wrestle with little kids b/c ur extra heavy & being in a swimming pool the water loosen ur muscles. I had plenty of the aquatic therapy in the swimming pool getting my therapy. I tried to hop in bed like a normal person & it almost ended up leading me into the nursing home with a broken hip... my mama would always have idle threats contingent upon me doing the exact opposite... For example, she will always say do this or else but she really wants u to do the or else part she wanted to put reverse psychology on ur mind. Lol I can deal with it... or maybe it's cause of me, when I was younger it was a stubborn, stupendous side of me that immaturity in not having a man in the household. U see, I have a father, I know my daddy, I've got a good relationship with my daddy, it's just is that my mom raised me & she did a great job too. It's just that no man was in the house. I was too busy instead of being a man of the house (btw, when someone came to the door & rung the doorbell I always took off running in the opposite direction, lol that was super funny, I would always make a b-line to my room, scared half to death) but anyway I was too busy trying to be the man **OF** the house instead of the man **IN** the house... I tried to take charge of everything. With my sister & my mom I was trying to police & boss the two.

I was a major stifles to them... Flickering the lights on & off, to arguments of teenage rage in punching holes in the walls. To answering the phone aggressively when someone called ma.

Yep I did it. I'm not proud of my behavior now. I was hellish back in the 5th-8th grade... I lived & I learned a lot. Music & serving God did that for me.. if it had not have been for those two things along with a praying. mother who was doing the best she could. Now don't put me in a box & throw away the key... I wasn't that bad now. Never in trouble with the law. Never a booster of meats shoplifter or nothing serious. Never into drugs or cigarettes... I was more of a black & mild kind of fella in high school & in college...

How does it feel?

When u ask me how I'm doing? I give u the obligatory customary, I'm blessed, black, & highly favored ... or the regular I'm fine. But if u were to ask me how I'm feeling the answer would welllll not so good. Now I know that this is the holiday season, people are happy, filled with glee, good energy around, I'm not one to bring this down but seriously I just have to speak on my feelings towards the holiday seasons & who is invited & who is not invited, who likes this person, who likes that, MY bigger question is ain't we some kin tho?

How I feel often

I feel lonesomeness even tho I may not be lonely... Yeah I may be there sitting in a corner by the door at the Christmas party But u know what's missing it's u. Or it's someone like u! I ain't gonna lie I been wishing, dreaming & praying for a sweet soul to enter my life for times like these. Www &: gatherings, a time when it felt brutal to me especially during these holidays & gatherings..I ain't had a significant other my whole adult life & not having someone gets u always noticed as just the dude who ain't got a girl. That part is normal I bet to see.o.. i always feel as I'm the third wheel, I have friends but every single one of them is married & kiddos who are taller than me now (when I sit in my wheelchair.) lol

There's So much more that I have to say, i'm not a writer, poet. I'm just saying step into my life a little. This could happen to anyone & I don't wish anything bad on anyone.

Before it's too late & there ain't nothing u can do about it now

I also wanted everyone to hear what I hafta say about how I feel sometimes lately especially at these parties & gatherings. & about other things as well. From my perspective it is true when people will say you don't get invited to many things especially either you're sick or you're dead and then if u do attend people overlook you, make you even wonder why did you even show up in the first place. Especially if u get overlooked... Makes you feel like a little kid...

It seems as if I get the obligatory "hey & bye" treatment at parties. People seem to just leave me at the bday parties, gatherings & other stuff don't just runaway & run upstairs & don't come back down to talk to me unless I send for u.. my booty can't have a change of scenery but urs can... lol. I can't help it, it was right there..but it's not just here at my daddy & Jearldine house... imagine being somewhere at a party in a room all alone while everyone else is upstairs & ur downstairs by yourself. U may be at the party but are u really tho? & I don't think that it's fair or bc I am outta the looped loop about what's going on with the family biz whether it be from who going overseas deep sea fishing, where & what's happenings for the holidays, etc. I would like to ask if just bc I have a debilitating injury I would like to be accounted for & included too.

Some people do make a room in their homes for you and your mom to sit in. And I thank you for that. But just because it's like that, still you get left behind looking at the bigger picture, when people go upstairs to sing happy birthday or to do something else party functioning wise. You always get left downstairs all alone. Just think about it if you were in the other person shoes how would you feel? Really it's like wow! That's what I mean about being at the party but you're not really AT the party. You left all alone in the room by yourself with the TV and it could be for various amounts of time because everybody else can go upstairs and you can't! And this time for them to socialize up top, but if I were to say something about it, I would be the individual in the wrong. So I don't say anything I just go along with the flow and be happy that I'm there, but again that's not a good feeling.

I'm more friendly to other people than some are. I'm nice to a lot of people, I'm kind, I'm personal, I'm so approachable, i I really do care about other people, and it really does exudes off of me. So I can't help if someone *halfway invites* family to a party, dinner, or cookout. I mean, you tell me what am i supposed to say when asked? What are you doing for the holidays? It's a whole lot of drama in my book because I don't know who likes who? Or who likes whatever it don't matter to me. So no, I don't subscribe to the negative stuff. Sorry... I use the noted scholar Buddy Loves philosophy, "ELE" =Everybody Love Everybody. But It's always said that "it ain't your house" or "get your own house". And you know what I say to that, "okay"because when I get back on my feet I can't do it right now but when I get back on my feet I'm going to build a huge compound. I can already see the vision. And we're going to do it every holiday at my house with all of my immediate family & a few friends. Just you wait and see it's going to happen

I said this to my Crawford family in order to unite, motivate & strengthen us;

It pretty much has come to my attention even closer., over the past 10 years since Grandma & Grandaddy passed away that we all have moved further & further away from the love that we bring to each other... Besides funerals, & the invitational dinner at Tellis & Stacee house for Thanksgiving & even then It seems like it's no more get togethers, reunion style gatherings, family game nights, visitations, vacations, viewing party for sporting events, etc & this was happening even before Covid so we can't say it's bc of Covid. But that can be debated... Some people would say u can't make some people get together, or unite, to counter that I will just say pray, & u make sure u put more effort into ur connection with ur family.

As I look & talk to other people in different states I wondered (while they are talking to me a thought bubble 💭 arises in my head) why can't my family be tight like this? We used to be real tight like that. Should I say something about this? Why shouldn't we gather? I wonder what Grandma would do & say? the cost of things shouldn't be a problem, locations shouldn't be a problem, timing shouldn't be a problem, now all we gotta do is add each other into the mix.

Did u know that cause I didn't know that happened like years ago...Stuff is going on that we don't know about. Now I'm not just saying this bc the past weeks ago was my bday dinner & only a few came thru to support, everyone says they had plans &. I understand this to a certain degree, & I have a really good question for everyone. Everyone is real quick like to make adjustments in their life for someone's funerals & or to be with their loved ones as soon as that person dies, & understandably so, but what about the times while they live... should u be proactive in their life, think about this for a sec... did u really do enough? Did u try ur hardest? Did u show ur love? what is the solution for this? I say that prayer changes things...

I can remember every holiday we would always serve dinner at grandma house & she wouldn't want nobody at her house, lol. Now I might be a little bit older for a birthday party or to have a holiday gathering but I think that there should be a priority for celebrating birthdays, holidays & special occasions... I know Brenda would definitely do something big for us, & would bring us the specialty dish of Mac & cheese with a key lime cake. & Greg would always "We too big shot for him", & here go grandaddy chiming in "Ummm Hummm", I just was curious can we keep & start up on traditions? I know that some would say it takes a lot out of u to host a dinner but there's strength in numbers, when u got family that can help u organize & clean up.... &

sometimes it ain't even got to be a big "shin-dig" Why can't it just be a fam event not just a one-person event, we are supposed to be family right? Some kinda get together so we can get together as a family & stick together.

Someone once told me to create my own family (like I'm in a video game virtually or something) idk if anyone else feels the way I feel about it, but after I hear what others do with their families It makes me wanna mimic them & try that with mine. But we don't do that. Well who says we can't? I'm open or we as a family are open to this...

Also I sent an unite & an. Inspiring note to my other family members; My immediate family: Rush, Belton, Hill, McNair, Buoy, Hamilton, West, Sims, Rowland, Leslie Family

(Long Read, well.... Long write-up for me at least, so it may be a short read for a normal human, lol)

It pretty much has come to my attention even closer., over the past 10 years since Grandma Connie died that we all have moved further & further away from the love that we bring to each other... Besides funerals, it seems like it's no more get togethers, reunion style gatherings, family game nights visitations, vacations, etc & this was happening even before Covid so we can't say it's bc of Covid. But that can be debated... There is No communication between anyone, or at least idk things, but speaking to some we as a outsider parts of the family not knowing or some do & others don't know about deaths in the fam or we could be somehow related & don't even know it. Some people would say u can't make some people get together, or unite, to counter that I will just say pray, & u make sure u put more effort into ur connection with ur family.

As I look & talk to other people in different states I wondered (while they are talking to me a thought bubble 💭 arises in my head) why can't my family be tight like this? We used to be real tight like that. Should I say something about this? Why shouldn't we gather? I wonder what Grandma wold do & say? the cost of things shouldn't be a problem, locations shouldn't be a problem, timing shouldn't be a problem, now all we gotta do is add each other into the mix.

Did u know that cause I didn't know that happened like years ago. Auntie Bucket has a doctorate now along she & Lee picked up & moved, Stacee & Tellis done moved along with Junior & Tina had a house built, alongside with 57 & Henry going to be on Giligan Island, lol so they bout to dip. Lee-Lee getting married and Keke did too celebrations happenings weddings, graduations, birthdays, etc... are these supposed to be a **secret.it** sure does feel that way.. to me it does. I'm also asking to known & be communicated on a little bit not just let me know after it's over and done with like I don't need to know the things that are going on right in the moments. Now I'm not just saying this bc the past weekend was my bday dinner & only one came out the fam. Everyone says they had plans &. I understand this to a certain degree, & I have a really good question for everyone. Everyone is real quick like to make adjustments in their life for someone's funerals & or to be with their loved ones as soon as that person dies, & understandably so, but what about the times while they live... should u be proactive in their life, think about this for a sec... did u really do enough? Did u try ur hardest? Did u show ur love? what is the solution for this? I say that prayer changes things...

I can remember every holiday Grandma Connie would always serve dinner at her house

& ur birthday was a holiday as well to her. Now I might be a little bit older for a birthday party but I think that there should be a priority for celebrating birthdays & special occasions... Whatever happened to this. Why did this ever die along with Connie? I just was curious can we keep up on traditions? I know that some would say it takes a lot out of u to host a dinner but there's strength in numbers, when u got family that can help u organize & clean up.... & sometimes it ain't even got to be a big "shin-dig" Why can't it just be a fam event not just a on- person event, we are supposed to be family right? Some kinda get together so we can get together as a family & stick together.

Someone once told me to create my own family (like I'm in a video game virtually or something) idk if anyone else feels the way I feel about it, but after I hear what others do with their families lt makes me wanna mimic them & try that with mine. But we don't do that. Well who says we can't? I'm open or we as a family are open to this...

This concludes our public service announcement about the family.

Family is everything, u should get to know all of them to find out more about who they are especially while u have a chance. In the words of the Notorious B. I. G "Well if u don't know, then now u know."

I realize that it could be so much worse for not only me, but for the experience that u may be going through as well. I just felt the need to bring these points up for mention. & now back to our regularly scheduled program… it ain't my bday but u can come over here & kiss me!

& speaking of kissing, I hadn't even kiss nobody in 12 years, the whole time I've been in a wheelchair. & imma not an inmate or in a hospital bed. But yeah I'd like to skip over my 30's it was a real not so good portion in my life. I felt like I'm just so incredibly late to the party for everything... it seems like everyone has been there & done that... Time is definitely of the essence...

Why someone in my position, would frequent the strip club so much!

Now I'm not saying that I would visit these establishments quite frequently or every chance I get, u only can assume I do, & u know what assuming does, ASSUME= ASS out U.M. E lol I learned that in school... But either way the reason is for only bc where else would a person get shown any love from. I mean u could go around different function with family & friends or maybe even at different church events u could put yourself out there it just seems that you'd only get any attention, love and affection from a warm blooded woman at a gentleman's club which that is what every man needs. I know, I know, I know everyone just wants to be my friend, & yadda, yadda, yadda, but u know what, u wanna be friends well I wanna be the friend alright, well I wanna be the friend that's "F'n u in the a$$", that's the kind of friend I wanna be, lol. (PG-13 version, I'm trying not to cuss, my elders & my mama gonna be reading this) Now when I spoke of this out loud one even offered to give me sex herself, but I would have to pay for it. did I just say that "Eerrrkkk, rewind that," yep that happened. A sex worker she was. Now no, I'm not a sick psycho with a perverted mind or a whoremonger or nothing like that. I was raised right, ok now. To serve & protect ALL women. I just am who I am... I can't help that women get attracted sometimes & wanna talk, I am just being me. But yeah it's been thrown up in my face... "Pushin P"- is what they say nowadays.I knew it wasn't nothing but a money grab, lol I'll just leave it at this, I'll leave it in God's hands...& he got the whole wide world all in his hand. But I met a Nice former stripper, (2yrs retired) age 27, from The Blue Flame Gentlemen's Club out of Atlanta Ga. Or better yet the other establishment known as Magic City, it was one of those clubs in the ATL. She was gonna do me like that movie "Pretty Woman" she told me. She was gonna buy me outfits dress me up & everything. I'm not lying either. U can ask my mom. How we met was through a dating app. & then another lady my ma met through the phone well she goes by Kendra Hawk, she wasn't a sex worker, she was a pure angel. She is a very nice woman. She met ma over the phone, as a matter of fact she is the reason why ma got a cash app. Before that she didn't even know what cash app was. She chipped in & helped out tremendously. It was beneficial & we definitely needed it. I lost contact with her during our move my phone lines were twisted... So if anyone knows her & is reading this please forward me to her, I wanna reach out to my friend check up on her & Laurie, so I can make sure she get her flowers before the 31st. Good friends are hard to have nowadays & the instant bond that me & Kendra had we vibe out real good together & the funny thing about it, we hadn't even met flesh to flesh, skin to skin, hugged or none of that made contact with each other, we had planned on it for sure after Covid-19 but we lost touch.

But back to the strip club. Sitting in a wheelchair "I'm already halfway there" lol Good vibes, good energy, good fun, real friendly environment/atmosphere, yeah u could probably do away with the whole nudity but in the strip clubs defense it's not like it is a big orgy going on... & don't get me wrong, sex is a part of human nature. Every man thinks of sex even the preacher does. How I know is bc one made a comment after prayer with me & my dad, he said well at least u got the activity of your limbs so u can stroke. & then he motioned his arm in a masturbation motion. O. K. I got an even bigger bombshell I'm not trying to disregard or dismantle morally what some preachers do but when u come into my home for prayer & then hand me a pornography dvd, I just would lose all moral but in the moment it was all laughs to me but I really sat back & thought about it. Did a preacher really give me a porno & said he had more if I needed... WOW & I didn't even know him like that. He came to the hospitals in Atlanta & Augusta to pray for me. Like I told u it was so many people, calls, cards, & flowers we should've had a registry or name tags where ma could remember who everyone names were & in her defense looking back at it. I didn't expect her to remember either she had so much going on & I was in a coma. But they had proof, she took pictures but anyway, I still didn't know him, I just know he was a chaplain or clergy maybe a minister...

It seems like I am cursed or something I do not know what it is. I must be under a hexa or something, I feel like I am really curse for real. And I'm not not really telling anybody any of this stuff cause it seems like so embarrassing, well embarrassing to me at least, but Oh my God really is this you, I keep asking myself, is this u I see in the movie bc it looks like something on Disney plus, but in my imagination I'm seeing it in the movie and realize it as well. But I cannot get a date the regular way and everybody is taken or they have babies everywhere I'm talking like three and four kids and stuff, I try and do the online and get a date through these dating services but the internet is filled with all these internet imposters or at least I attempt to buy a date, (I actually was not going to do that by the way) that option is still there. it pretty much has me checking myself, is my mind playing tricks on me. What in the world is it? At the time of this writing I am 40 years old and I haven't been on a date in 13 years, I'm not ugly, when you turn on the TV everybody else got a relationship, and I ain't never really had one. What is going on? Many questions will arise from me? Is it me or is it the wheelchair do I need to change my appearance or do I think of something I mean what is it really? By the way Mama just heard me talking to my book, she chimed in and said pray to God.

To be all honest on this what does this have to do with my life and my experiences? Well a real reason is because a man needs a woman, being disabled or sick you don't have the ability to go out and seek one or do you have limited view it may be a limited option for you. It's all going downhill once you get sick. If you're married yeah that's until death does you part, but if you're not married why you're fixing to catch hell, and I know from experience about this too and from fellow victims as well, who's the whole lot of friends too.

But there is somebody out there that's just for you, you got to always believe it, I always have good faith, and trusting God that he'll make a way because eventually "If you can't do for one, you can certainly do for another. Somebody in this world wants you." Wow, thanks grandma! U always told me that.

And the meantime while you wait, me personally I don't see anything wrong with someone like me going up inside of a strip club gentlemen's club. Lol

But back to the sex in the strip club topic.

No sex there in the club. The late great Gerald Levert even made a hook to. a Chris Rock song about it, "No sex in the champagne room". Now at the hotel after they clock out, ummmmm. Lol I'll just say commence ur conversations... lol The ladies are actually human beings & in the art world they know how to dance, doing cardio workouts & planking on a pole, it's just the same as if a husband & a wife a dancing seductive to each other. In my book she would get two thumbs up who says u can't talk or u can't go to the gentleman's club? People would judge u. Or if u go to Hooters or Juggs, I mean I wouldn't take kids into sports bars anyway. But I see family's in there. But to me it's like are you strong enough in your convictions & ur beliefs. I know I am. I've been tested too. but there is a saying,"The flesh is WEAK!" But mine ain't & on that note, I'm gonna leave that there. Lol I'm gonna leave it riiiigggghhhhtttt there, lol

Would u look at the time...

Speaking of time man while I'm thinking of time, time is precious... Take advantage of everything u have right now., I may have all these crazy asinine doctors & prescription bills, but u know what I am still blinking & breathing... All in all man just treat people right... don't bother everyone cause u don't know their story & if u wanna know just ask & listen to them, everyone is going through something... Be kind to everyone, bc u just never know.

Shoutout to all my fam too. It ain't just only my mama (even though she is a big contributor in my life.) others assists. Daddy- Darriek Rush, Sr. I hope I make u proud on this one. Actually I know I made u proud. Tell me though, boost my ego a little bit I wanna hear u say it, lol u know, if u say it 3 times in a mirror I appear like Candyman in the mirror, lol or some money might fly from the sky & rain on top of ur head... I put this on e'erythang I love u bruh! Jearldine Rush- "The world's greatest stepmama" u da' best! U need to open ur own kitchen & start charging for plates. Lol, nah I take that back. Don't cook or work no more, u can sit it on down & just tell people what to do. Take a load off young lady. lol. My favorite & only Irish Twin Sister Stacee (were only 10 months apart in age) & Bro. In law Tellis Leslie (my brother from another mother, lol) (now we talking about a Jack of all trades for real) shoutout to y'all & my fam Ash, Aubree, & TJ. Pepo, Todd, Zuni, Lady Z, Tia, What up doe? Lol Shoutout to e'erybody, I ain't finna go down my family tree list of all my kinfolk, lol they know who they are! But let me not go any further without acknowledging that I do have cousin who is my 57th cuz, I know, I know, I know, 57, I wonder it's down there so low, she might have disowned me & stopped claiming me to be related nowadays. She might not know me no more since a distinguished Dr & all. But nevertheless her ma is still my Auntie Jackie & that is that.

"FOE"= (Family Over Everything) Ride or die! 💯

Anyhoo.....

So that's my story & I'm sticking to it.

I don't have a ending to this yet & that's a very good thing bc that just means that I'm still here. but one of the docs said that I probably won't ever walk or be the same again... Well, nah u know I'm not believing that... he must not know my God, we will just prove that theory wrong... & ma already said she would take me ANYWAY shape or form... More to come. But I leave u with...

My strokes memoir

While everyone is out, enjoying their life on most weekends, well, in my life I'm a part time introvert more of an ambivert. I will fall & bust my head (to the white meat, lol) if I get out my wheelchair... Or go anywhere that's not handicapped accessible. it's normal bc my mom is disabled herself, so it's like that when u don't wanna bother anyone else or be a burden on someone else's plans. My homeboy's daddy died & the first thing I thought about doing was to drive over there to be with them in their time of bereavement but I almost forgot that I c—— wait, I won't use the negative "C" word. I can just say, not at this time... but I almost forgot, & I had a dream & a vision that I could walk & drive one day... it was amazing. I don't know how long in the future but future me please, lol

I can be reached thru email at Keith.rush10@Comcast.net or just come by the house, that is, if I know u, but u better call before u come &

don't just pop up over out the blue cause we are paranoid about people we don't know & ur best bet is my email **Keith.Rush10@comcast.net** I promise I won't bite.... YET!, lol pfffffttttt HaHa. Bite u like a dog on a chicken bone, lol. I have a go fund me under the name Krusher's prescripts & things are ridiculous. & a cash app: $tilmanmac

Thanks for all that you can help with if u help, God Bless U

Sincerely, Keith "Krusher" Rush

More to add about my mom...

Sweetness, also known as "Ma", "Mum", In my British accent "Muvah" lol. Whatever I call her I know one thing for sure, I don't know what it is about mama but she always mentioned a synonym or a present tense term for marriage. She will always ask you about your significant other in hopes that you are living happily ever after. She always looks out for the other person. She always wishes a couple well no matter who they are. She always wants to see others enjoy their lives & it doesn't even matter... Ma is a whole complete angel as a earthly human being. And gentlemen I give u my blessings I will immediately relinquish her over to u, yes, she is single too, insider information, so take it from me, she's a keeper. So with that stated I know she want to get married for reasons to have a significant other to make you whole and for love, companionship, a real romantic loving relationship, that's why she would wanna get married, well me too, lol well at the right time If it ain't me she's trying to get married, it's whomever she comes into contact with. You see ma been trying to get me married since I was like 10 years old lol. It›s always been the main topic of conversation with other people. If it ain›t hope for others, its hope for herself too. And most people would tell her «the grass ain›t always greener on the other side» & I would rebuttal that by saying «Let her be the judge of that»

I just gotta say shout out to Mom & Dad for having sex & creating me, lol, hahaha. They created my sister first though. I don't have any kids now I keep telling Mama that I will have my own family, just you wait you will see. Which it's only right that I keep getting asked the same questions over and over again, where is your wife? Where are your kids? 6Ain't it past your time for you to have somebody now? Sometimes that thing just hits a little bit different when is your mother asking you those questions. It's all right though she knows my answer every time, my answer is "when God says so, then it is so" enough said after that.

I see exactly what she means all the time when she says she needs a man around the house. She did say she needs a husband to do a lot of things around the house. Like the things that would be needed to clear up a house & I usually would be the one who does it but with me and want to do all of the necessary stuff around the house. All of the chores and the load of my new things that a man would do like empty trash, maintenance on the car, keep the cars cleaned up, you know simple solutions would do. I used to be the one who drive for her. I used to take her somewhere everywhere but now she takes me everywhere. And she does not even like driving at all. And you would not catch her driving over a bridge at all. That's our worst fear. And she don't drive far or anywhere she doesn't know so I'm limited to where I can go, unless somebody else takes me. And especially now all she ever drives for to take me to the doctor or to go pick up a drive thru order, even then, she only go when there during the hours of no traffic, not busy hours of the day meaning not the traditional hours and only in the daytime.

Remember how I said that being on the ventilator was no fun, also having a tracheotomy and a feeding tube is not the coolest either but I can recall the time when I was in Walton rehab and of course since I'm a mama's boy my ma would feed me some grits knowing good and well I'm not supposed to have any of that solid stuff. Lol.

Meet the author:

I am Keith "Krusher" Rush. (Have no fear, Krusher is here, well ALRIGHTY THEN, lol) Krusher is what I usually go by, I answer to both names Keith or Krusher... & Krusher is my name for real. I promise u, it's not made up like a stage name or nothing... I know it sounds like I'm some type of rapper or artist or some kind of sports phenomenon or something... pfffttt i wish, lol... But I am from Thomson, Ga. Born & Raised. Thomson High School class of 2000...shout out to my Dogs... Graduated from The Art Institute of Atlanta. An honorary wannabe member of Omega Psi Phi Fraternity Inc. (Woof-Woof Throw dem' hooks up!) The accomplishment & fulfilling of the accuracy of the depiction from my stories are all true... I don't have an extensive background as an author or a novelist, I'm just using a gift from God to bless the readers. I actually have never written before but after receiving rave reviews from others God told me to go on & share it around the world...

with that being said, i've seen so much and more is to come in my life. A love to many, just on the lookout for true love in whatever shape or form it comes in. Loves all sports. & is enthusiastic about my new beginnings into this writing realm. I'm not a real author, & don't claim to b, like all the big wigs out there, I'm just doing my thing & writing it down. God is good I appreciate him letting me be here. & just like God I truly am a nice man who shares it all with the world, so please buy my memoir, I owe people money, lol

*India Hall was an inspiration, Mama was my day to day regulator, & finding Gabriella is my motivation! Quick story about Gabriella, when I was in coma I remember hearing her say her name in my ears & she walked away, I can remember opening my eyes to get a glimpse but all I saw was a shadow. (That must've been jelly, cause jam don't shake like that, lol hahahaha :) Okay, I added that "jelly" part for laughter... lol. But Gabriella is my Cinderella, & I gotta find her, "so have no FEAR, KRUSHER is here" stand by baby I am on my way!

Sincerely,
Keith "Krusher" Rush

...

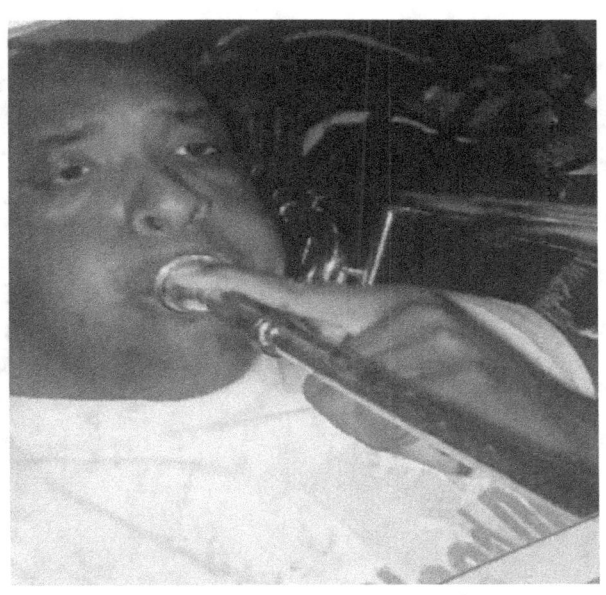

www.ingramcontent.com/pod-product-compliance
Lightning Source LLC
Chambersburg PA
CBHW071220070526
44584CB00019B/3090